In the name of God

***

Unwithering Flames: Book-5 "Shaheed Janbuzurgi; Narrated by His Wife" by: Haleh Abedin
Copyright © 2023 Green Palm

All rights reserved. No portion of this book may be reproduced in any form without permission from the publisher. For permissions contact: info@greenpalm.net
Translated and edited by: Green Palm books
Cover by Hussein Reza Vanaki
First Edition

To contribute in the publishing process and be informed about other volumes of the series, please contact: info@greenpalm.net

Unwithering Flames

—— Book 5 - Janbuzurgi ——

In order to have a fruitful and prosperous relationship, it has been aknowledged that love is an essential component. Unfortunately, the meaning of true love has been lost. Many have relegated love to mere intimacy between a man and a woman. However, this is just the initial stage of true love, and we must aspire to reach a higher level beyond physical attraction. Such love is built on the foundation of honesty, enjoyment, selflessness, and spiritual attainment. Although many strive to reach this transcendent form of love, the affairs of this world become a barrier for them.

This series of books entitled Unwithering Flames recounts to us stories of those men and women who, in the events of the Islamic Revolution and the Iraq's war against Iran turned away from this world only for the sake of God. In doing so, they became lovers in the true sense. They had the type of love that did not just make the pain of this world bearable, rather it was something beautiful for them. The love whose flame has not dimmed even with martyrdom or death.

 www.GREENPALM.net
 +98 999 99 16 140
 info@GREENPALM.net

Saeid Sanbuzurgi

Birth: March 3, 1966
Entering University of Art: 1992
Marriage to Zahra Saburi: December 15, 1992
Martyrdom: July 12, 2002

SYNOPSIS

She married a photographer so that each moment of their life would be captured. However, when they opened the camera after the wedding, and no photographic film was inside it, she came to realize that this life wasn't going to be anything similar to her imagination. Life with someone who had taken pictures of death for years and whose distance with death and life was equal, was way sweeter than her previous speculations. So sweet that she has not yet believed Saeid's departure.

Contents

Chapter 1
Fahimeh's Letter to Her Husband................9

Chapter 2
A Prosperous Girl........................19

Chapter 3
An Unwanted Partner..............................45

Chapter 4
Hajj Behind the Lens..............................63

Chapter 5
Sons Die and Fathers Live........................75

Chapter 6
Patience, Lady Zaynab's (a) Gift..............103

Chapter 1

Fahimeh's Letters to Her Husband

Iraq's imposed war on Iran commenced as I was celebrating my religious coming of age. I used to go to the ladies' Basij[1] office in the mosque to lend them a hand. They would say, "Do not touch anything, just sit in a corner and watch." I would sit next to them and do exactly that. They used to tailor

---

1. Basij consists of volunteer forces who were formed in Iran during the Iraq-Iran war, alongside the Islamic Revolutionary Guard Corps and the Army of the Islamic Republic of Iran in defense of Iran against its Ba'ath enemy. After the war, this force still plays a role in various fields in which widespread participation of people or public services are required.

soldiers' clothing in one corner and package canned fish in another. And in the end, they would line up the boxes at the mosque's door for the pickup to come and load them for the war front. The war lasted so long that later on, I had abandoned sitting in a corner and did not need anyone's permission to help.

I graduated in sciences from Kowthar High School in Nazi Abad,[2] and I was eager to go to university. I read a lot of history during high school, including the history of Islam. After graduation, I took the university entrance exam without any delay, but unfortunately, I failed. I came to know that the Ministry of Education was employing hourly-paid adjunct teachers. I attended the interview and was accepted. On the first day of autumn, I went back to the classroom. I was a temporary teacher in the second grade for a few months, and when their teacher returned, I went to teach the third grade.

It was fall in name only, hence the schools were open, but the summer's heat was still strong. Uncle Majid and his wife

---

2. Nazi Abad is a neighborhood in southern Tehran.

had just moved from Shahriar[3] to Tehran. When they settled down, we went to their new house one night with Mom, Dad, and my other siblings. We knocked on the door a lot, but no one opened it. There were no mobile phones back then for us to contact them, so we took a taxi and returned back home. Upon entering our alley, we saw my uncle and his wife. They had also come to our house, and we were not there. They, too, were about to go back. Despite our insistence, they refused to come in. Right there at the door, my uncle said they had come to make an offer of marriage. He sought Dad's permission to come with his friend one night. He had a great deal of trust in his friend. My father said, "If you say that they have faith in God and the Prophet (s) and that our characters and social statuses are close to one another, then there's no problem. Let them come." They made the arrangements for the proposal ceremony.

Only my uncle and the groom came for the proposal ceremony. I was in the kitchen. Mom repeatedly cued me to prepare the tea, but I was playing for time. Each time

---

3. Shahriar is a city in western Tehran province.

a person came or called for a proposal, I would tell my mother to send them away. I had prohibited them from even informing me if someone phoned regarding a potential match. I didn't want to get married, let alone with a member of the IRGC.[4] I thought the members of the IRGC had weird expectations from their families. For this reason, I wasn't keen on serving them tea, lest they thought I was interested in getting married. But this time, the one who had come to propose was my uncle's friend. Thus, out of respect for my uncle, I felt forced to go and serve the guests. I took the tray of tea and reluctantly started on my way. When I got to the entrance of the living room, luckily my younger brother came and took the tray. I greeted our guests and sat beside my mother. A pleasant fragrance pervaded the entire room. I breathed deeply and took in the air. The TV was on ; I

---

4. Islamic Revolutionary Guard Corps (IRGC), or Sepah, is a military and cultural organization, which was established about three months after the victory of the Islamic Revolution of Iran (in April 1979) under Imam Khomeini's advisement to protect the revolution and its achievements and to cooperate with the army of the Islamic Republic of Iran.

turned my head towards it. I pretended to be captured by the news and, until the end of the meeting, didn't turn my eyes away from the TV. I didn't turn to see how the groom looked and what clothes he was wearing. I didn't even take a look to see whether he would appeal to me or not. Later on, after we were married, he asked me once, "On the day of the proposal, did you not strain your neck from staring at the TV so much?" I felt embarrassed. I said the TV program really captured my attention, I didn't tell him I wasn't keen on getting married.

When they said "*Ya Allah*"[5] as a sign to leave, Saeid came forward and asked for my school's address. I was looking downward. All of a sudden, I caught sight of his socks which were extremely clean for a man. As he came closer, the aroma of his fragrance got even stronger. The fragrance he was wearing was Tea Rose. He used to apply Tea Rose or Damask Rose perfumes on a daily basis. His clothes were fragrant all the time.

---

5. "*Ya Allah*" (literally, O Allah) is a phrase used to address God. The term is used by Iranians as a forewarning. For example, when a stranger or *non-mahram* intends to enter a private place, he says "*Ya Allah*" to declare that he is about to enter the place.

He said he was going to bring me a book; a biography. He wanted his future wife to be like the lady in the book. Thus, it was agreed that if I read the book and liked it, then they would come back for further talks.

The weather was still warm. When he handed me '*Fahimeh's Letters*' I caught a glimpse of him for a moment. Beads of perspiration were visible on his forehead. '*Fahimeh's Letters*' was a collection of letters written by Fahimeh and her husband during the war. Fahimeh was a Quran teacher; her husband was a soldier. Their marital life was confined to these few letters. Saeid and his friends had found Fahimeh's grave, coincidentally in Behesht-e Zahra[6] Cemetery. They found her martyred husband's testament in the glass box above the grave and published it in the *Jomhouri-e Islami* newspaper. A few days later, Fahimeh's family called the newspaper office. Saeid asked about Fahimeh, and they handed the letters of Fahimeh and her husband to Saeid. I read the book. It was agreed to inform me of the next meeting via the school's phone.

---

6. Behesht-e Zahra is Tehran's largest cemetery, where many martyrs of the Islamic Revolution, martyrs of the Iraqi war on Iran, and many other Iranian political and religious figures are buried.

We talked with each other three times; each of those times he came by himself. Our expectations matched one another. We would start from these commonalities, and our conversations would become prolonged. And each time my uncle's laughter from behind the door would bring our talks to an end. "No...Their talks are not going to finish." Saeid and my uncle were in the same battalion and Saeid worked in the battalion's publicity department. He was a photographer, painter, and a caricaturist. My uncle said the comrades in the battalion showed him a lot of suitors for marriage. He was well-mannered and educated; moreover, he would perform his prayers and fasts on time. He had gone to a number of matchmaking meetings upon the recommendation of his friends, but none of them appealed to him. The last time, he had seen a VCR player[7] in a girl's house, and according to him, he had run away. My uncle realized that he was looking for a god fearing, religious and politically aware girl. He had spoken to him about me. He had said that my brother's daughter might be a good match.

---

7. Back then in Iran, having VCR player at home was regarded inappropriate for religious families.

Saeid was the baby of the family. All his siblings were married, and they no longer prompted him to get married. When they realized that he didn't care, they left the issue to him. He was reticent before his friends and his family. He never informed others when he was wounded. During the war, his mother had seen him in her dream that his legs were lifted off the ground and he was soaring towards the sky. She had reached for his hands and saw that his face was injured. The next morning, they called every hospital until they finally found him. His father had told the nurse that he was one of Saeid's friends. If he had said otherwise, Saeid wouldn't have come to the phone.

Shrapnel had hit his ears and impaired his hearing. However, during those times, his camera was constantly in use. Saeid couldn't tolerate staying in the hospital. As soon as he regained consciousness, he would plead with the doctor to sign his discharge forms.

Once, he brought me his photo album of Halabja.[8] He told the story of each photo

---

8. Halabja is a Kurdish city in Iraq. Saddam Hussein launched a chemical attack on the city in 1988,

in detail. It was horrible. For a long time, the thought of Halabja did not leave me. The things I saw in those photos, Saeid had seen with his own eyes. He had also suffered from the chemical weapons there.

On a Friday in the fall, when the weather had gotten a bit colder, Saeid's sister came to our home. Saeid's and my ideas had become so similar. It felt as though we were compatible for one another. . He had sent his sister to see if anything was left unsaid. When she called my name—Maryam, I said to myself, "How careless of me; I think he is one of those men who says something today, but he forgets it the next day." He had told his sister, "She is your namesake." All his family members visited to decide on the *mahr*[9] and agree upon the time for when the marriage solemnization was to be recited. Only his father was bedridden in the hospital and thus, wasn't able to attend. It was agreed that the *mahr* should

---

because of its support of Iran during the Iraqi war on Iran. In this attack, approximately five thousand civilians were killed, and as a consequence, the area became uninhabited.

9. *Mahr* is the money paid or owed by the groom to the bride at the time of marriage.

be fourteen golden coins and the date for the recitation of the marriage solemnization to be determined by office of Ayatollah Khamenei[10] They had also brought an engagement ring with them. But Saeid and I bought the wedding ring together. It had twelve gemstones. I said, "As a sign of the twelve Imams." He laughed and purchased it. He didn't like wedding rings. He didn't allow us to buy him a ring, a watch, or even a shaving machine. He only accepted a small wallet.

---

10. Ayatollah Khamenei, the present supreme leader of the Islamic Republic of Iran since 1989. Prior to his current role, during the Iraqi war on Iran, he was the country's president.

Chapter 2

A Prosperous Girl

We got engaged on October 15. The ceremony was held in our home. I was wearing a white dress and he was dressed in a bright color. He disliked dark colors. He always had a few ironed bright shirts in his closet. He would wear them during the week, and wash and iron them on Fridays.[11] He was very careful with all his clothes and belongings.

Haj[12] Azarmi solemnized our marriage. He was the Imam of the Tolid Daroo

---

11. Friday is the official weekend in Iran.
12. *Haj* or *haji* is a person who has performed the *hajj* ritual. The title is often used before a person's name, mostly as "*hajj*." In the Iranian culture, the term "*haji*" is also used to address a man respectfully.

neighborhood mosque. He liked Saeid just like his own son. All the people in their locality liked Saeid. He had become dear to everyone ever since he had painted the photo of Imam Khomeini[13] in the mosque. We were standing in the corner of one of the rooms on the ladies' floor and were surrounded by women. I was shy of Saeid, and Saeid was shy of me and the other women. When *Haji* came, the women left the room. We sat on the floor, and *Haji* sat in front of us. When he was reciting the vows, our eyes were busy looking at the carpet's flowers. Once the vows had been recited, the women started clapping. I looked at Saeid. It was the first time I was looking at him from close up. His cheeks had turned red. He was uncomfortable among all those women.

When the ceremony finished, Saeid called me from the landing. I sneaked my head out of the room door, "We will talk with each other later." He said, "Come, I have brought you a gift." I ran towards the stairs. He gave me his gift quickly and went.

---

13. Ayatollah Seyyed Ruhollah Musawi Khomeini (1902-1989), known as Imam Khomeini, was the leader of the Islamic Revolution and the founder of the Islamic Republic of Iran.

It was a book, *A Ray of Prayer Secrets*, by Mr. Qaraa'ati. He had written on its first page, "Dedicated to my pious and dear wife." Afterwards, I couldn't sleep all night. My mind was constantly thinking about Saeid. I was sure that at that point, I was the most prosperous girl on earth. I had lost my heart to Saeid; to his manner. My heart missed a beat at the thought of him having fallen in love with me. Before long, I was missing him.

We bought two notebooks—one for myself and one for him. Every time we wanted to see one another, we would write a sentence for each other in the notebook. A verse of the Quran, a sentence from Nahj al-Balaghah,[14] a narration from the Holy Prophet or Imams (a), a line from the martyrs' testaments, or any other comment which could be useful and helpful in our life. Those notebooks were so dear to our hearts. Each day, our eyes and ears were chasing good words and quotes to write for each other. It was the Eids of the month of Sha'ban,[15] We

---

14. Nahj al-Balaghah is a book containing the sermons and letters of Imam Ali (a), the first Shiite Imam.
15. Sha'ban is the eighth month of lunar calendar. Some of the happiest anniversaries of Shi'a are also in

had gone to a *hei'at*[16] together. Saeid's jacket had big pockets where he used to keep the notebooks. That night, one of the notebooks fell out of his pocket. We only realized this when we had already arrived home, and I was getting off the bike. He felt glum. The notebooks were of great importance to both of us, but I consoled him. I said it was no use crying over spilled milk, and we could get new notebooks. He was so sad. "I wasn't responsible," he said. Finally, I managed to convince him to get another notebook the next day and to write for each other again.

The radio used to air Ayatollah Mazaheri's[17] speech every night at nine o'clock. His speeches were about the etiquettes surrounding marital life, mutual respect, mutual understanding, and the like.

---

this month, such as the birthdays of Imam al-Husayn (a), Imam al-Sajjad (a), Imam al-Mahdi (a), and Abu al-Fadl al-'Abbas (a).

16. *Hei'at* is a religious gathering to commemorate the Prophet's infallible household usually on their martyrdom or birth anniversaries.

17. Ayatollah Hussein Mazaheri (b. 1933) is a Shiite authority and the head of the seminary of Isfahan. Ayatollah Mazaheri is known as a morally committed figure of the seminary.

Saeid had told me to be next to the radio at 9 p.m. wherever I was and to listen to the program. He, too, would listen to it whenever he had free time. The radio was my old friend. We used to sleep in the yard on summer nights when I was a kid. By 10 p.m., we were all in bed waiting for Dad to turn the radio on. We loved the *Night Story* radio program. To us, it was like a lullaby. From early evening, we were all eagerly waiting for *Night Story*, and when the story would begin, we would fall asleep.

Saeid had a motorbike. But I dreaded motorbikes. Four days after the proposal meeting, he came to school with his bike, "Hop on and let's go for a ride," he said. I was still rather reserved around him. I pictured for a second that I would be sitting on the back of his bike with my hands wrapped around his waist, and Saeid would be riding fast on the road. The wind would be blowing through my *chador*,[18] causing it to blow up like a balloon. The wind turns into a storm and throws me off the bike in the middle of the road.

---

18. *Chador* is a long cloak-like garment, which covers the entire body, worn by Muslim women in Iran and some other countries in public places.

"I don't get on motorbikes," I said.

He pressed his lips together to avoid dissolving into laughter. He had understood that I was afraid of the motorcycle.

"You might ride fast, and I will be thrown off into the street," I said.

He was now laughing openly. "You get on; I will ride slowly. Just take care of your *chador*, lest it gets caught into the wheels," he replied.

I hopped on. I sat behind him, leaving a distance between us, and gripped his jacket firmly with both my hands. As soon as he took off, I immediately wrapped my hands around his waist. It was nearing *adhan*[19] time, so we went to the mosque and performed congregational prayers. He never missed the timely congregational prayer, as long as he was well. It would make no difference if we had guests or were invited somewhere; he would apologize to the guests and go to the mosque for his prayers. If we were on the

---

19. *Adhan* is a call for Muslims, which informs them of the time of prayer. It is often cast or recited through minarets of mosques.

street, he would ask for the address of the nearest mosque and be present at the time of *adhan* in the prayer line. We performed prayers together at many mosques around the city.

I had a sudden craving to visit the mausoleum of Shah Abd al-Azim.[20] I wanted a couple's pilgrimage. I, who was scared and avoided motorbikes for twenty years, now said, "Let's just slowly and carefully go to the Holy Shrine of Shah Abd al-Azim for pilgrimage." We changed the direction of the motorbike towards Rey.[21] Saeid was born in Rey. We stopped by Mr. Fakheri's house en route. Heidar Fakheri was a close friend of Saeid's. On the frontiers, they had made an oath of brotherhood. If one looked through Saeid's photo album, they would find it filled with photos of the two of them together. Their graves are also close to each

---

20. Abd al-Azim al-Hasani (789-866) was a great grandson of Imam al-Hasan al-Mujtaba (a), and a prominent companion of the ninth and tenth Shiite Imams. His mausoleum in Rey is a major place of pilgrimage in Iran.

21. Rey is an ancient city of pilgrimage in southern Tehran, where the shrine of Abd al-Azim al-Hasani is located.

other now. Heidar was martyred during the war. We had paid a visit to Heidar's home without prior announcement. They received me as if I were their own sister-in-law. After that, we would ask about the well-being of Fakheri's family at every occasion. Whenever they saw Saeid, it was as if their own son had come back to life.

Saeid had promised to buy me a gift if I memorized Surah al-Waqi'ah. As soon as we arrived at the bazaar of Shah Abd al-Azim, I recited the Surah al-Waqi'ah, and he bought me a black velvet headscarf right then and there. He didn't like headscarves in the beginning. He had asked me to wear a *maqna'eh*[22] everywhere. Now that he himself bought me a headscarf, it meant he had trusted me with my *hijab*.[23] When we arrived home late at night, everyone was sitting at the dinner table. Mother was waiting for us to arrive to serve dinner. "Why

---

22. *Maqna'eh* is a particular kind of headscarf for women, which covers the head, the neck, and chest.
23. The term *hijab* is mainly used to refer to a religious covering in the presence of *non-mahram* men. To maintain *hijab*, women must cover their body and adornments from *non-mahram* men. Of course, they do not need to cover their hands up to the wrist and their faces.

are you so late?" She asked. We had already eaten kebab and basil in the Shah Abd al-Azim neighborhood. "Let's sit and eat a few morsels," Saeid said. After Saeid left, I showed everyone the headscarf. "Why have you charged him at the very beginning?" Dad said. "That's necessary, Dad," I replied. My father laughed. "Poor us, sitting here all hungry and thirsty, waiting for you to come, not knowing you were elsewhere."

On the first Thursday of each month, we would go to the Reminiscence Night meetings of the Hoze Honari,[24] and on Fridays to Friday prayer. He would be waiting for me in front of the school's entrance at twelve noon if I had a morning shift; and when I had an afternoon shift, he would come at 5 p.m. and we would go to a mosque. We used to travel to mosques of further distances so that we could spend more time with one another. We used to frequently visit Behesht-e Zahra and the Holy Shrine of Imam Khomeini, too; however, we wouldn't go there by bike. Saeid used to say riding on intercity roads was

---

24. Hoze Honari (lit. Department of Arts) affiliated to Iran's Islamic Propagation Organization.

hazardous. The very first time that we went to Rey by motorbike, we did it with utmost care. Once he borrowed his friend's pickup for us to go to Behesht-e Zahra on Friday and then to Friday prayer. I put on my clothes early in the morning and waited for him, but he didn't come. I called their house, but his mother said he had left the house a while ago. Finally, he arrived. His hands and face were black like that of Haji Firooz's,[25] and a very large exhaust was present in the back of the pickup car. He was on the way to pick me up when suddenly, a giant thing from under the car hit the ground in the middle of the street, and thud! Behind him, the street had become chaotic. The cars behind him were trying to overtake one another to avoid hitting the exhaust. Saeid got out and put the exhaust on the back of the pickup truck with a lot of effort. He washed his hands and face, and we set for Behesht-e Zahra without the exhaust.

The phone was ringing constantly, as

---

25. Haji Firooz, a man who according to Iranian folklore darkens his face and hands with soot and wears red clothes, and from a few days before Nowruz until the end of it, he tries to make people laugh with his movements and recites ballads.

soon as our line was connected, especially on those days when Saeid had exams, and we were away from each other. Most of the time, it was me who called him at his office. He used to say, "The telephone belongs to the *bayt al-mal* (public money); it is sinful to use it for personal purposes."

We went to the cinema no more than a couple of times. He used to watch the movies on television, Channel One, on Fridays after the children's program. He liked our war films, but he used to say that half of them were not real; they made it up themselves. He was saying this as someone who had witnessed the war firsthand. But among these movies, *The Glass Agency*[26] and *From Karkheh to Rhein*[27] were different for him. The first time that The Glass Agency was broadcasted, Saeid silently shed tears in

---

26. *The Glass Agency* is a 1998 Iranian film written and directed by Ebrahim Hatamikia. The film is about Abbas, an Iranian veteran of the Ba'ath regime's chemical attacks on Iran, who is about to die because of his injuries from the war.

27. *From Karkheh to Rhine* is a film written and directed by Ebrahim Hatamikia about the fates of some victims of chemical attacks by the Ba'ath regime on Iran.

front of the television. I came to realize the meaning of his tears only after his health condition deteriorated, like Abbas (*The Glass Agency's main protagonist*).

In December, the students' first semester exams started. I always had to be with the students at the time of examinations. I was concerned the wedding ceremony would coincide with the students' exams. When I mentioned this issue to Saeid, he became resentful. He had made a vow to recite fourteen thousand *salawats*[28] if we could make an appointment with Ayatollah Khamenei's Office. He said that if Ayatollah Khamenei was unable to recite the marriage, then he would be wistful forever. It wasn't nice that despite this fact, I was simultaneously worried about my students' exams.

My birthday was approaching. My mother-in-law later told me that despite their insistence that he buy me a gift, he didn't agree. He would say, "I don't want

---

28. *Salawat* is an honorific prayer uttered by Muslims when they hear the Prophet's name by which they send peace and blessings on Muhammad (s) and his Household (a).

to. It's not necessary." But he had been busy with something in his room and whenever someone opened the door, he pushed everything under the bed, so nobody could see what he was up to. On December 12, he came to our home with an armful of gifts.

"This is on behalf of *haj khanum*.[29] This is on behalf of *Haji*. This is on behalf of my sister. And this..."

The last one was from him. He had made a postcard using a pasteboard, colorful papers, and a battery. As soon as I opened the card, the lights in the card turned on, and music started playing. There was a quarter gold coin in it too. Musical postcards had not yet found their way to the market. It was his own idea. He had quite an exquisite taste.

We always gave each other gifts on our birthdays. Saeid usually presented books and cards. The least he used to do was to draw some flowers on the book's corner and write a sentence. But it never happened that we threw birthday parties or took photos. I

---

29. *Haj khanum* is a respectable way to address women in Iran.

thought about throwing a party too late. By then, Saeid's disease had exacerbated.

Finally, an appointment was made for our marriage solemnization with Ayatollah Khamenei's Office. It was for December 15 which was coinciding with the birth anniversary of Lady Fatimah (a)[30] and Imam Khomeini. We arrived at the Rahbar's office at eight o'clock in the morning. It was raining, and you could smell the scent of the soil. The air had a vibe just for lovers. I had a weird feeling. I wasn't sure if it was stress or intense eagerness. As I breathed in the scent of the soil, I started feeling more excited in my heart. I was truly delighted. We were eleven couples. The brides were set in one corner of the room and the grooms in the other. When Ayatollah Khamenei entered, the bride's whispers dominated the room. Everyone shouted with great excitement, "*Salle alaa Muhammad, Farzande Zahra amad,*" meaning, "Peace

---

30. Lady Fatimah al-Zahra (615-632) was the daughter of the Prophet (s) and Lady Khadijah, the wife of Imam Ali, the mother of Imam al-Hasan, Imam al-Husayn, and Lady Zaynab (peace be upon them), who was titled as Umm al-A'immah (the mother of Shiite Imams).

be upon Muhammad, the son of Zahra (a) has arrived." I remembered my friends' and relatives' requests for prayers. Before reciting the marriage solemnization, he talked about the life of Imam Ali (a)[31] and Lady Fatimah (a) for a few minutes. He advised us to teach religious issues to one another. He recommended that we give small dowries, throw small parties, and accept little *mahr*. All the *mahrs* were fourteen gold coins or less. He said, "Reciting the wedding vows for those who have contented themselves with only one gold coin is more pleasing." His last words were for the brides and grooms. He said, "You two are the principles of life. Try to gain each other's satisfaction." After a while, Saeid placed both of our photos next to each other in a photo frame and wrote this sentence below it.

Ayatollah Khamenei was the grooms' representative, while Mr. Mojtahed Shabestari was the representative of the brides. We would appoint them as our representatives, and they would recite the vows. On that day, the first marriage

---

31. Ali b. Abi Talib (a), known as Imam Ali, is the first Shiite Imam and the successor of the Prophet (s).

solemnization was ours. I was really nervous because of the responsibility I felt on my shoulders. I started uttering *dhikr*[32] under my breath. As soon as the marriage solemnization was done, everyone started to recite *salawat* and congratulated us. We sat there until the vows of the other couples were recited. When we came outside, it was raining heavily.

It was a custom that the groom's family send a gift for the bride on the night of Yalda.[33] Our Yalda Night was a week after the marriage ceremony. My uncle and his wife were with us at our home, and we were all waiting for Saeid. The ground was covered with snow. I had butterflies in my stomach. He was never late, except for the time when the pickup's exhaust had fallen

---

32. Muslims often remember God by repeating and reciting phrases such as Lā ilāaha illā Allāh (There is no deity except Allah). These phrases, which are reminders of God, are called "*dhikr*" (literally, remembrance).

33. Chelleh Night or Yalda Night is the Iranian traditional festival celebrated on winter solstice which is the longest and darkest night of the year. It corresponds with the night of December 20 or 21 in the Gregorian calendar.

off. We ate a little food out of anxiety and cleared the *sofreh*.[34] I was pouring tea when he arrived. He had gone to the hospital to visit his brother. Since I was still resentful, I took the students' exam papers and busied myself with them. Dad criticized me. "After all, Saeid has come, my darling daughter. Leave those papers and come sit next to your husband." He had brought three bracelets with him. When I wore the bracelets, he stood up. "*Ya Allah...*" He disappeared before my dad and uncle could get up to give him a ride home. They went looking for him in the street, but it was as though he had dissolved into the snow. The next day, he said he had hidden behind a lamppost. He could not sleep at night, if he felt he had put a burden on others.

On January 24, he came to our home with a big present. He said, "Congratulations." It was neither of our birthdays, the birthday of any of the Imams, Mab'ath,[35] or any other Eids. "Congratulations for what?" I asked.

---

34. *Sofreh* is a cloth or polymer piece spread on the ground or table when having a meal.
35. Mab'ath, or festivity of Prophet Muhammad's (s) first revelation, is the anniversary of Prophet Muhammad's (s) appointment to prophethood.

"Today is the one-month anniversary of our marriage," he said. And he handed me the gift. He had printed a big picture of Ayatollah Khamenei and had framed it. I stepped forward and kissed his face out of delight. All his acts were done properly for the right circumstances.

It was upon us, in fact upon me, to set a date for the wedding reception. He had said to my father, "I will wait as long as you and Zahra want." However, I was aware of his true feelings, though he never revealed them. He used to miss me too. We were getting quite attached to one another. He would cut his work hours and university classes short to come and see me. I would accompany him to the door when he wanted to leave in the evenings, but we could not say goodbye. We would talk about anything, even irrelevant issues, so that we could be together a bit more. As soon as he would turn the corner of the alley, I would miss him.

My father said, "The dowry will be ready by Eid al-Fitr."[36] Eid al-Fitr had coincided

---

36. Eid al-Fitr is a major festivity for Muslims, which is held after the month of Ramadan on the first day of Shawwal.

with the Nowruz holidays[37] that year. Saeid and his mother came to visit us on the second day of Nowruz. They brought a ring and a bolt of *chador* fabric used for prayer. I tried on the ring upon Saeid's insistence. The ring was loose on my finger. We went to the jewelry shop via motorcycle and exchanged it for a smaller one. We were invited to my father-in-law's house for dinner. March 26 was chosen for bringing the dowry to our house, and April 1st for the wedding reception.

He didn't allow my father to buy the wedding suit, since it would only be used for one night. He wore a jacket and pants at the proposal ceremony. He said he would give it to the launderette and would wear the same thing again. Dad sent me on a fool's errand, and I don't know what he said to Saeid that convinced him. We took money from Dad, and the two of us went shopping. He chose a dark blue suit—the ones worn by much older men. I think he didn't even wear it

---

37. Nowruz is a big celebration of the beginning of the solar year (Persian calendar), which is held every year on the first days of Farvardin (the first month of the Persaian calendar) in Iran and other countries that were part of ancient Persia.

five times after the wedding. His university invited us to a ceremony to introduce the top student. He gave me his suit jacket at home and wore a jacket. He wore his suit jacket only when he went up on the stage and took it off immediately after that.

Saeid believed in the wedding banquet. We served lunch for our wedding. After the ceremony, we had *aroos-keshan*[38] to Saeid's father's house. Our home was on the second floor. It was my decision to be next to his parents. After all, he was a member of the IRGC, and I wouldn't be alone if he were to go on a mission. We entered the house under a shower of *noqls*[39] and chocolates. The guests were also following us when Saeid asked his mother to stop the guests for some time. He brought a pitcher and a laver and took my shoes and socks off. He put my right foot in the laver first. When he poured water, it felt like he was pouring

---

38. *Aroos-keshan* is a traditional practice performed by Iranians after the wedding, in which the family and relatives of the bride and the groom take the bride to the groom's house with particular ceremonies.

39. *Noql* is a small confection produced in various sizes and flavors. In Iran, *noql* is a symbol of happiness. There is an old tradition of throwing *noqls* on the bride and groom in weddings.

water on fire. My feet were burning because of the high heels I was wearing. I touched his shoulder. "God bless you," I said. It was a misunderstanding on my part however, he wasn't only relieving my pain. He said he was following Imam Ali's advice; "Wash your bride's feet and pour the water around the four corners of your house. It is a blessing for life." When he dried my feet, the guests came forth.

For our honeymoon, we went to Mashhad[40] for three days. We had taken our notebooks to write down some of Imam Reza's (a) quotes for each other. These writings continued for a couple of months after the wedding. Saeid had a lot of work and lessons to study and did not have time for writing. However, I still continued writing for him. He had bought Dr. Mazaheri's books for me. Since he was short of time, I used to write a summary of those books for him in the notebook. When the number of summaries increased, he prompted me to adorn the outlines with colored pencils.

---

40. Mashhad is a city in northeastern Iran, located in the center of Razavi Khorasan Province. The city is home to the mausoleum of Imam al-Ridha (a), the eighth Shiite Imam.

We would lend the notebook to whoever was soon to be married among friends and relatives. It was filled with life lessons.

In our first couple of weeks together, we were invited to the homes of our relatives for *pagosha*.[41] Saeid was not really keen on lunch or dinner parties. Far from being a recluse, he was quite outgoing and liked visiting relatives. But he didn't like troubling others for lunch or dinner. He was quite busy. He did not stay for dinner in our house even during the one-month engagement period. It was great suffering for him when my mom would offer him fruit and tea. We had an argument or two because of him not staying with us. However, I stopped insisting when I realized this was his character. We made the parties shorter, only to have tea.

The final exams had ended, and we had given out the report cards. I did the housework and went to the Quran class. One day he asked me a question.

"What would you do if I asked you not to go to school anymore, and I will work more to afford all expenses?"

---

41. *Pagosha* is an Iranian tradition in which the newly married couples are invited to the relatives' houses.

"Then I won't go."

He couldn't believe it.

"If this makes you happy, I'll resign," I said.

He was really happy. He was of the opinion that working outside the home reduces the vitality of women. Around the same time, one of my colleagues had demanded divorce. Her husband had the same demand as Saeid, and she had said, "Either job or divorce."

The first days of my pregnancy coincided with the cold season. I would sit next to the heater and read '*Nine Months to Motherhood.*' Saeid had bought the book. He had also purchased many other books about the upbringing of children and their food and clothes. As soon as he would get home, he would pick up a book and ask questions. He would glare at me if I didn't know the answer as a sign of penalizing me. But I would misuse the smile in his eyes and would complain, "It is not a school lesson that I have to learn by heart, line by line." He wouldn't listen to me. I had to learn the ins and outs of childcare by heart.

I wouldn't sit at any table; had the host not paid their *khums*.[42] If someone brought *nazri*,[43] I would eat after asking about it. He was really committed to such issues. He used to say *halal* and *non-halal* food affects children even in their mother's womb.

I used to recite the Quran daily. When I was busy doing something, I would play Abdul-Basit's[44] *tartil*[45] recitation. Before sleeping, I would caress my baby and recite recommended Qur'anic chapters for him. I maintained my *wudhu*.[46] And after he was born, I fed him milk while I had *wudhu*.

---

42. *Khums* and *zakat* are financial obligations in Islam.
43. *Nazri* food is a meal served for free by Shias on the anniversary of martyrdom or birth of infallible Imams, particularly during the days of Imam al-Husayn's (a) martyrdom.
44. Abdul-Basit Muhammad Abd al-Samad Salim Dawud (1927-1988) was a famouse Egyptian reciter of the Quran who has many fans and followers throughout the world.
45. *Tartil* is a method of reciting the Quran in a measured pleasant tone.
46. Wudhu is a ritual ablution of one's face and hands, and wiping one's head and feet in a particular manner. In Islam, wudhu is required for the validity of the prayer and some other acts of worship.

It was before *fajr adhan* when I woke Saeid up. I said, "Get up, let's go to the hospital." He couldn't believe the time for delivery had come. I said, "Let's go. If it's false labor, we will return." He agreed. We said our morning prayers and got on the motorbike. As soon as they checked my pressure, they gave us the admission note for being hospitalized.

Muhammad Sadiq was born just as the *muazzin* uttered "*Allahu Akbar*" of the *zuhr adhan*. We hadn't informed anyone. I was alone, and Saeid had to perform his prayers. When they told me, "Your son is healthy," I immediately began to cry. The voices of the *muazzin* and Muhammad Sadiq's crying were mixed with each other. I turned my head towards the window, and a tear rolled down from the corner of my eye onto the pillow.

Two hours before visiting time, we informed the families. The grandmothers and grandfathers became furious, "Do you two think you are abandoned and have no one?!" they said. But, when they saw their grandchild from behind the glass, they forgot about their complaints. I had not yet seen him. Saeid was imitating his hand and feet movements, and I was laughing uncontrollably. He was beaming with joy. My mother-in-law felt embarrassed in front of the others due to her son's childish acts. Saeid was joyful in a way that was never seen of him before.

We went to my father's house straight from the hospital. Saeid was neither staying properly nor was his heart letting him go! He came and left with sadness so many times until I returned to our own home on the third day. He had prepared the bed for his son and put up a mosquito net. He would help me out whenever he was free. He would say, "Give me his cloth diapers, I will wash them." My mother would not allow it, saying, "This is the grandmother's job."

Saeid chose the name himself, "Muhammad Sadiq." Before our marriage, he would also tell whoever would have a child to name their child Muhammad Sadiq. When we gathered with his friends, there were three to four 'Muhammad Sadiqs', so we would address them with numbers!

Chapter 3

An Unwanted Partner

Saeid had a constant earache. It was due to the shrapnel that had hit his ear. The nerves of his ears were damaged. It would make no difference whether his surroundings were noisy or not; he always had a whistling sound in his ears. At nights, Muhammad Sadiq would wake up and would not calm down until he had whatever he wanted. Saeid had headaches, but he never complained. Only sometimes he would say, "Is something wrong with him? Why isn't he calming down?" Saeid had to leave the house at five-thirty in the morning, and some nights Muhammad Sadiq would be restless until sunrise. The cry of Muhammad Sadiq or any other child used to bother him, both because of his headache and for the child's sake. After all, a child can't speak out to unburden their heart! He would always become heavy-hearted, due to the crying of a child.

I did not like sitting in one place. Even the promise of a Kachiran sewing machine could not make a tailor out of me.

When Muhammad Sadiq started crawling, Saeid's father made a baby walker for him. My father-in-law was a retired railway employee. We used to call him Haj Aqa. After retirement, he would work with wooden planks in the basement. He made so many toys for Muhammad Sadiq. In the afternoons, our house would become a wrestling venue. Saeid and Muhammad Sadiq used to wrestle. If I felt like it, I too would join them. When Muhammad Sadiq was in the walker, Saeid used to recite poetry and encourage Muhammad Sadiq to chase him. He would call Muhammad Sadiq, "O my little goat! O my little goat!"

The house was old, and the vents were connected to each other. Our neighbors above and below us were not likely to be in peace! For the poor fellows below us, we were like an earthquake. My sister-in-law would stand by the cooler vent on the upper floor and used to laugh uncontrollably at Saeid's recitation of poetry.

The joking and laughing were for ourselves. In front of strangers (*non-mahrams*), neither I would joke with Saeid, nor would he say anything to me. What happened at home would remain inside the house's four walls and would not get out. He would neither speak of anything from our house to anybody nor did he like to listen to the private stories of people. The fact that his colleague at the workplace would share about his wife and describe certain things would enrage him endlessly. Due to this, many people assumed that Saeid must also be a serious and humorless person in his private life. He was serious, but he wasn't humorless; he was serious and responsible. If I entrusted a household chore to him, he would do an even better job than me. If he was cleaning the glass, I had to beg to get the cleaning cloth from him. I used to say to him, "Do not do something that would cause me to not ask for your help ever again!"

He would always say, "Islam is the religion of moderation; neither extremism nor apathy!" His character too, was as such. Everything of his was in proportion and in the right place. Going to mosque, *hei'at*, *azadari* (mourning), and *sinazani*[47] had their place; and rejoicing, celebrating, and banquets had their place as well.

Muhammad Sadiq learned to walk with the help of the flower at the center of the carpet. He would get up and go in circles, until he became all dizzy and fell. Once I counted how many times he circled around the flower; fifty-three times. He was the grandson, and everyone fell for his walking and gestures. Saeid's level of happiness was so much that it was equivalent to the joy of all of the others, put together. He really fell for the sweet actions of Muhammad Sadiq who had learned a nursery rhyme, "O my good and modest father, I am gratified being by your side." As soon as he saw Saeid, he would start sweet-talking. He had recently learned the chapter of al-Tawhid.[48] Saeid

---

47. *Sinazani* or chest-beating is a traditional ritual of Shiite mourning ceremonies, in which a maddah (eulogist) recites a poem with a certain rhythm, and mourners beat their chests in harmony with the eulogy. Famously, the practice is inherited from the mourning practice of Arab women in the early Islamic centuries.

48. Chapter al-Tawhid or al-Ikhlas is the 112th chapter of the Qur'an. It is titled in English "Sincerity" and composed of four verses.

himself taught him small chapters of the Quran. If he could recite from memory, there was a reward.

It was the night before the new year of 1997. Saeid said, "I want to go to the south to find work. Will you also come?" We packed our bags and set off. The family of Mr. Saburi-Zadeh was also with us. We went to Ahwaz[49] by plane. From there, we went towards Andimishk[50] by car. Not much time had passed since we had entered the highway when suddenly, the car broke down. Mr. Pazuki returned to Ahwaz on foot and returned with his neighbor's car. In Andamishk, the men were separated from the women. We were the guests of the Pazuki and Mahmoudwand families. Mrs. Pazuki's room was big. She had emptied half of it for Mrs. Saburi-Zadeh and me. Sometimes, one of our husbands would come and take us to

---

49. Ahvaz is a major historical city in Iran and the capital of Khuzestan Province in southwestern Iran. It was the main headquarters of the Iranian army in the Iraqi war on Iran. It was a target of frequent missile and air strikes of the Iraqi army.

50. Andimeshk is a city in Iran, located in the southwestern part of the country in Khuzestan province.

show us the neighboring cities. After three days, they again sent a car. Saeid had said, "Let us go to the garrison of Dokouheh".[51] We were in Dokuheh for five days. There were very few people there. They would not even constitute a congregational prayer. If the caravans of Rahiyan-e Noor[52] came, we used to gather with them in the *hussayniyya*[53] of Haj Himmat and recite congregational prayers. Some of the caravans held programs including the recitation of prayers and eulogy (*rozeh-khani*)[54] which we used to attend. The paintings on the walls of the garrison and the *hussayniyya* were painted

---

51. Dokouheh is an area near Andimeshk in Khuzestan province, which is home to one of the biggest Iranian military bases. During the Iraqi war on Iran, Dokouheh military base was the main operational base in Khuzestan.

52. Rahiyan-e Noor (literally, "the passengers of light") are caravans of passengers, who visit parts of Iran formally engaged in the Ba'ath regime's war against Iran. They visit western, southwestern, and northwestern parts of the country.

53. *Hussayniyya* is a place where Shias perform their denominational rituals, particularly mourning rituals for Imam al-Husayn (a).

54. *Rozehkhani* is a mourning practice in which the tragedy of Imam al-Husayn (a) and other Infallibles (a) are recited.

by Saeid. They were the paintings of the commanders of the war. He had done those paintings twelve or thirteen years ago, when he was a part of the Publicity Department of Battalion 27 named *Hazrat-e Rasūl*. He became acquainted with Ehsan Rajabi and Ali Uzamaiyan next to those very walls. They were all only sixteen or seventeen years old at that time.

The men had gone for *tafahhos*.[55] They only sent a message that if we liked, we could join the caravans which were going to visit the regions of war. We would go there if the kids were not in a bad mood. There was no bathroom, and the toilet was a 300-meter distance from our room. The conditions were completely warlike. Again, a message came that we have to mount the morning bus to Khorramshahr.[56] The men were

---

55. *Tafahhos shuhada* or search of martyrs is the search for the remained corpses of *shuhada* in war zones. Until the end of 2022, corpses of more than 45,000 of those missing in action during the Iraq-Iran war were found, but 2600 warriors are still missing.

56. Khorramshahr is a large city in Khuzestan province, southwestern Iran. During the Iraqi war on Iran, the city was occupied by Ba'athi forces for nearly two years, and more than one thousand of its Arab

there. We reached them when the cannon of the New Year was fired. Saeid's job was to take pictures of their *tafahhos*. We went to Tala'iyeh[57] together. They had placed the martyrs side by side. We took permission to recite prayers and Ziyara Ashura[58] for them. I felt tranquil. As if I had lost someone and they were now by my side.

Saeid took Muhammad Sadiq and me to *tafahhos* a couple of times. Saeid would take photos while we observed. They would dig up the ground with a mechanical digger. If they reached any water container, plaque, or other items like that, they would switch off

---

and non-Arab people were killed by the Iraqi army. In 1982, the warriors of Islam liberated the city in Operation Beit-ol-Moqaddas.

57. Tala'iyeh is an area in the west of Khuzestan province in Iran, near the Iran-Iraq border. During the Iraqi war on Iran, the Iraqi army repeatedly launched chemical attacks on this area. After the war, corpses of many Iranian soldiers were uncovered in the area, where a monument was built for them. The area is frequently visited by caravans of Rahiyaan-e Noor.

58. Ziyara Ashura is a salutatory supplication addressed to Imam al-Husayn (a), the third Shiite Imam, which is recommended to be recited, particularly on the Day of Ashura.

the excavator, and a person would remove the soil with their hands. I saw from a close distance that they dug out a martyr from inside the ground and wrapped him in the flag. When Saeid wanted to take pictures I was by his side. I saw with my own eyes that when he unwrapped the flag, the face of the martyr was intact. It was hard for me to believe, even though I had witnessed it with my own eyes. Saeid had gotten used to this. No scene was more heart-wrenching for him than the scene of Halabja.

In August of last year, he had also gone for *tafahhos*. I had no news of him for one month. Before he left, the pain in his kidneys had increased. I was clueless, and there was nothing I could do. When he returned, the sun had scorched his skin. When he recovered from the exhaustion of the journey, he started to describe his experience, "I was going towards the guys, and suddenly there was a sound of an explosion two meters away from me. It was a mine."

Muhammad Sadiq was still one month short of turning three, when Saeid went for *umrah*.[59] It was a new custom to enroll university students for *umrah*. From the very beginning, there were too many applicants. However, nobody would show any insistence on going. Although it was called 'drawing lots,' in fact, it is God that invites you. Saeid's name came out in the very first year. He had also won the title of top student and apart from *ziyara* of Mecca going into his share, he also attained a journey to Syria as a reward. In the summer, he went to Mecca, and in the winter, to Syria.

He had gone to the market to buy the clothing of the *ihram*.[60] The shopkeeper, who had figured out that Saeid would soon be a *haji*, started pulling his leg by saying, "One who goes for *hajj* has to have a belly. His belly should fall down over his belt, layers upon layers, just like this," and was indicating to his own belly with his hand. "You do not possess such a belly to become a *haji*." Saeid too, had said, "This is all I can

---

59. *Umrah* or *umrah mufradah* is a ritual performed by Muslims to visit the Ka'bah, but it is not part of *hajj al-tamattu'*.

60. *Ihram* clothing is a particular white piece of clothing that is worn when performing *hajj* rituals and visiting the Ka'bah.

do!" The shopkeeper was joking with Saeid and was not giving him the clothing. He didn't know that excessive work and the hidden pain resulting from the chemical attacks were not allowing him to gain weight.

Before leaving for *umrah*, Saeid took me and Muhammad Sadiq shopping. He said, "Buy all that you need for this month." He did not want us to have any insufficiencies and to be compelled to trouble anybody else on account of that. He never let me go alone to purchase anything. I never went shopping in my father's house nor in our own house. When Saeid had come to ask for my hand in marriage, my father had told him, "My daughter has never gone shopping up until now. Her mother and I buy all her things." Saeid too, had said, "I also do not like the lady of the house to go out for shopping. Whatever work she may have, I will do it for her." We used to go and buy things together. We would usually go on Fridays and buy things at once for the following one or two weeks.

All of us went to the airport to say farewell. After kissing his mother and sisters, he reached me. When he came towards me, I placed my hands upon my face and said, "O my God! It is not decent Saeid!" A cheeky smile appeared on his face. "Who will know that you are my wife? They will think that you too are my sister. Do you not want to kiss the face of a prospective *haji*?"

Whenever I called him *haji*, it would upset him. He used to object, saying, "What is *haji*? Say, *haj agha* or *agha* Saeid. Don't call me *haji*." But *haji* was easier for me to pronounce. Thereafter, when he saw that his opposition was not working, he let it be, and I would call him *haji* without any concerns. He used to call me Zahra *khanum* and would not drop saying *khanum*. He would always address us with respect. He had advised us not to put up any banners. We also asked our relatives, friends, and acquaintances that they should not put up any banners and lighting. Once or twice, when they came and stuck the banners up, we put up a ladder and removed them. On the eve of his return, we checked the whole alley several times to ensure there were no posters or banners on the wall.

We took a car and went to the airport. It was still dark when we returned and reached our alley. My eyes fell upon the door of the house. Two banners had been put up. *Haji*

got upset. "Didn't I say to not put up any banners? Didn't I say I don't want anybody to know?" And we too were completely clueless! No matter how many times we said that we did not put them up, nor let the others put them up, he still was not convinced. I squinted and saw that the names of his friends were at the bottom of the banners. When we had gone to the airport, they had come and stuck the banners up. As the guests arrived and crowded around him, he forgot about the banners. He was exhausted and soon fell asleep.

Guests were coming and going for two days. His sister and I were in charge of distributing the souvenirs. He had brought three bundles of cloth for *chadors* and a lot of shirts for men. We were cutting up three and a half meter pieces from the *chador* cloth, placing them in a bag with one men's shirt, and arranging them in a corner. Saeid started to describe his photography in Mecca and Medina before getting his photos printed. As they arrived in Mecca, he was restless, and for the first two days, he had done nothing; but then onwards, every time they went to the Ka'bah,[61], Baqi'[62] or Masjid al-Haram,[63] he would put the straps of his camera around his neck, trying to pick a spot where he would take advantage of the crowd in the sanctuaries and take a picture right in front of the CCTV cameras. I understood the difficulty of photographing in front of the CCTV cameras when I had the privilege to go on a pilgrimage. I had seen Saeid's pictures, and I understood where he had taken each photo. Before leaving for *hajj*, he sat down with me and taught me when to take the camera and how to hide it. He would not give his camera to anyone. However, he gave me one of his small cameras. His camera was my rival wife.

His last advice was that when I am about to see the Ka'bah for the first time, I should close my eyes and start praying.

---

61. Ka'bah (the House of God and the qibla of Muslims) is located in Masjid al-Haram.
62. Baqi' is the first and oldest Islamic cemetery of Madina where four of the Shi'a Imams (a) and many other noble Sahaba and the Tabi'un are buried.
63. Masjid al-Haram is the most sacred mosque located in Mecca. The mosque is especially venerated by Muslims.

I did not have guts like Saeid. When the police took my friend's camera, my heart started pounding. I almost gave them my camera voluntarily. We returned to the hotel, kept the cameras in the trunk, and continued with the pilgrimage, leaving photography aside. As soon as we reached Tehran, he took the camera's film for printing. There were no more than a few photos. He saw those few pictures and said, "How artfully you have taken these pictures! You wanted to compete with me?!"

Saeid used to talk to God from behind the lens of his camera. His pictures in of themselves were the pilgrimage. From his photos of *umrah*, he printed a number of brochures. He gave them to the Hajj and Ziyara Organization, too. They not only liked them but revered them. After that, Saeid became the photographer of the Organization and attained his aspiration. It is said that when you look at the House of God for the first time, everything that is in your heart is granted. It had been in Saeid's heart that he should go to the House of God every year. From that point onwards, he was a guest of the House of God every year in the season of *hajj*.

The first *hajj* coincided with our family moving to another home. We had found a house in the same alley. We moved our belongings and arranged everything at the speed of light. He wanted to ensure that we were comfortable. The city was in the vigor of Nowruz when he left. During those days, the duration of *hajj* was forty-five days. Sometimes, it would even become fifty days. It was so long that Saeid would send letters and call.

With some of Saeid's friends, we visited each other's families. The wife of one of his friends had delivered a few times before, but none of the babies had survived. Her twins were born together and died together! When Saeid called, he said that he supplicated by the side of the Ka'bah that Allah grants them healthy and righteous children. I said, "*InshaAllah*."[64] When Saeid hung up, that very friend of his called. He asked about how Saeid was. I said that he was busy with his pilgrimage. He wanted to give the news of him becoming a father to Saeid. They had

---

64. *InshaAllah* (literally, if God wills) is a common phrase in Muslim dialogs, often used to show what one intends to do in the future as long as God's will is factored in.

become parents on Imam Reza's (a) birth anniversary and named him Amir Reza. *Haji* returned home after the Eid holidays. We booked a hall and arranged a banquet. When Muhammad Sadiq went to sleep, I would serve tea for both of us and sit in front of Saeid with my hand under my chin! He would tell me about the acts of *hajj* and the places he'd been to. I used to listen to it all and developed a longing. He had fallen in love with 'Arafat.[65] His photos of 'Arafat made one remember the Day of Judgment. It was as if he had photographed the Day of Judgment, itself.

One time during the storytelling, he suddenly jumped from his place as if a bee had stung him! He had remembered one of his *tawafs*.[66] In that *tawaf*, a compatriot woman had glued herself to his side and circled the Ka'bah with him. However much Saeid distanced himself from her, she would keep reducing the gap. Eventually, Saeid had

---

65. Arafat is a land in eastern Mecca, sojourn in which is a main part of the rituals of *hajj al-tamattu'*. *Hajj* pilgrims stay in Arafat on Dhul-Hajjah 9.
66. *Tawaf* is one of the *hajj* rituals in which the pilgrims circumambulate around the House of God for seven times.

gotten angry. "Respected lady! Keep your distance!" Out of the blue, the lady also said, "Don't you know that during the rituals of *hajj*, all are *mahram*[67] to each other?!" Saeid too said, "So, come and mount my shoulders then!" His anger was due to the fact that because of the altercation with that woman, his attention had gotten distracted from *tawaf*.

After the visitations of Nowruz, he sat down to complete his thesis. The title of his master's thesis was 'Photography in War.' I also assisted him. He read his writings out loud and if there was any problem with the content or it did not convey the intended meaning, he rewrote it. We would review the typed texts one more time to ensure there were no spelling or editing errors. Muhammad Sadiq had also grown, and he did not bother us. He would either ride his bicycle in the yard or would busy himself with his toys.

---

67. When a man and woman are *mahram*, they do not need to observe *hijab* in each other's presence.

Chapter 4

Hajj Behind the Lens

During the days of the *hajj*, we saw Saeid less often. The Hajj and Ziyara Organization used to put up an exhibition of carpets, handicrafts, and pictures of *hajj*. They had to select and print the pictures for the exhibition. He was working day and night. Photos were like his children. He took care of them and got concerned about them. And all of this was even before he was sent for *hajj*. When he returned, for a long time he would be preoccupied again. When he was finished with printing the photos, he used to take the negatives and contacts of the photos to the Hajj and Ziyara Organization and archive them there. *Hajj* was for forty-five days, but they would have at least one meeting per week during the year. They would scrutinize the photos, organize programs for the exhibition and plan for the following year.

He went to his second *hajj* with Mr. Rajabi, his close friend. One of the photographers had to stay due to some issues and Saeid had introduced Ehsan Rajabi in place of him. Ten days before their departure, the pain in his kidneys intensified. The pain was constant, similar to the ringing in his ears. Until his martyrdom, I did not know that his kidneys had also been shot with shell fragments. Later, Mr. Rajabi showed me a picture in which shell fragments had created a hole in the flag which was in Saeid's hand and had hit his side. The picture was taken by Mr. Rajabi himself.

During the same time, he caught a cold too. We went to the hospital. Whatever tests they ran, the cause of the illness was not found. He stayed home the remaining ten days and rested before leaving. To go or not to go had nothing to do with his kidney pain. If God wills, he can cure it within a night; it happened as he wished, and Saeid got better and was able to go.

The closest photos to God's House were always taken by Saeid. My heart would miss a beat when he described how the path would be opened for him through all those pilgrims. It seemed that he was one of God's chosen ones! Otherwise, it was not easy to reach the Ka'bah. His words made me imagine performing *tawaf* around the Ka'bah while wearing the dress of *ihram*. Saeid, who had guessed what I imagined, got upset as he did not have enough money to afford to send me for *hajj*. The Hajj and Ziyara Organization paid the expenses of his *hajj*; therefore, it was considered a work trip. Eventually, he sent me for *hajj* in 2000. I did not agree to go alone. My heart was with Muhammad Sadiq, Saeid, and my home! If my child missed me, who would calm him down? What would happen to Saeid's headache and earache? How could I go to a foreign country by myself? After all, I did not know Arabic. More importantly, my heart wanted Saeid by my side! According to Saeid, all of these were just excuses. He said that he would take care of all these matters and that I should not be worried at all. He also said that God willing, I would find a good roommate and would not be alone. After all, I was making my trip for *hajj*, leaving all excuses and scenarios behind. When I arrived, I forgot all about home and life in Iran. My days and nights were passing in supplication and pilgrimage. Saeid knew that he would not find me in the hotel during the day; he used to call in the middle of the night. He also used to wake Muhammad Sadiq up to speak with me. I was not worried about them. Our journey lasted only fifteen days, yet Saeid sent a letter! Muhammad Sadiq too, had drawn flowers around the edges of the paper. I found good roommates, and we became very close friends. I didn't experience even a moment of loneliness. When I returned home, Muhammad Sadiq was doing fine, and my home was in good form as well. Saeid was right. All of those factors were only pretexts.

Hajj does not bring about tiredness, but even before the sweat of the journey had dried, we started packing up our belongings because the IRGC had given us a house. We decided that Saeid would pack up his things, and I would gather the other paraphernalia around the house. Saeid's belongings alone were equivalent to two or three sets of dowry. As he threw his papers and photos on the ground, they would transport him into the past. There were pictures of Halabja, *tafahhos*, and *hajj*. When he saw the pictures of his comrades, he was reminded of the frontier. When I became tired, I sat beside him, observing. When he brought out a picture of a martyr, his eyes became wet with tears. I packed everything else, but Saeid's room was still cluttered, so we moved a few days later than the specified time.

Muhammad Sadiq was a first-grade student. *Jashn-e shukufeha*[68] coincided with the first day of Rajab.[69] They were to give us the keys to the house on that very day. In the morning, we both took Muhammad Sadiq to school. Saeid had brought his camera and was constantly taking pictures of his son. When the students went to their classes, the parents left. We then went to collect the keys to the house. Saeid and my brother took most of our belongings to the house, while fasting. It took us two to three weeks to settle down. When Saeid was around, he did Muhammad Sadiq's dictation himself. I was in charge of his other lessons. The first three months, we were exasperated by him. He would spell a letter correctly and then an hour later he would forget it. We thought

---

68. *Jashn-e shukufeha* (literally, celebration of blossoms) is a festivity exclusive to first-graders at primary schools for their first day at school.
69. Rajab is the seventh month of the lunar year.

our child had some kind of defect. When the teacher arranged the first meeting, we were relieved. All the mothers thought that the problem was in their children! However, the teacher said that the first few months of school were supposed to be like this. They assured us that very soon the children would come out of this state of stagnation. And that is exactly what happened. Muhammad Sadiq's spelling progressed very soon. The reward for every twenty marks (full marks) he achieved was either fifty *tomans*[70] or Gorji zoo biscuits. First, he would play with the zoo animals to his fill. He arranged them on a plate and made them fight with each other. And when their limbs got thrown off, he would make a morsel out of them. However, the situation was not always that merry. When he would not learn a lesson, Saeid reprimanded him. I had no right to interfere. We had decided that whenever one of us reprimanded him, the other should not intervene.

During the anniversary of the Iranian revolution in 2001, he went for his third *hajj*. I took Muhammad Sadiq and went to

---

70. The Iranian currency equal to 10 Rials.

my mother's house. All the women of the family had come. We wanted to cook the farewell pottage for Saeid. Nobody knew that I was pregnant with Fatemeh. Even my mother and my aunt were oblivious. When the heat of the pottage subsided, we poured it in disposable plastic bowls. We then added fried onions, fried garlic, whey and fried mint leaves and arranged them in fives in big steel trays. As it was usually the case, they handed me the tray. I was wearing a *chador*. I gathered the corners of the *chador* and tucked them under my arms. Up until the fourth floor, I was moving the tray from this hand to that hand so that it didn't put pressure on my waist. If Saeid was there, he would have definitely reprimanded me! When the distribution of pottage was complete, I unwrapped my *chador* and spread the *sofreh*. When I bent down to spread the *sofreh*, my aunt found out. She grabbed my wrist, took me into the room and reprimanded me. I had been exposed! But my aunt did not tell anyone. That very year, my elder uncle and his wife were traveling to Mecca. Saeid had given them the address of his hotel, so that they could meet with each other there. Saeid had taken a lot of momento photos of them. The photos from the year 2001 were the last *hajj* photos of Saeid.

It was Friday, June 28. I had put the food on a mild flame of the burner, so by the time we returned from Friday prayer it would be ready. I don't know what busied us that we couldn't go for the prayers. We performed prayers individually and laid out the *sofreh* for lunch. It was past noon and I hadn't checked my blood pressure yet. Two months ago, as advised by the doctor, I had to check my blood pressure every day. My mother called and we decided to go to the park at night. Saeid said to go to the Najmiyyah Hospital to get my blood pressure checked and from there we would go to my mother's house. We had a car. As soon as he would get behind the wheel, he would switch on the car stereo. He had a tape of Muhammad Esfahani[71] and some Quranic tapes which he had bought from Mecca. He was not much into music and songs. When we were invited to weddings, out of respect to the host, he wouldn't refuse. He had advised that I should sit with my back to the center of the gathering and distract myself by reciting *dhikr*. He would busy himself in the same way. Generally, we used to go at the end of

---

71. Muhammad Esfahani (b. 1955), is an artist of Iranian traditional song and music.

the gatherings when everyone sat in their places and it was time to eat dinner!

After the nurse took my blood pressure, the doctor examined me. They said, "Walk fast in the yard for one hour and then come back; we need to admit you. Your blood pressure is high." I went to the yard disoriented and confused. Saeid and Muhammad Sadiq were busy playing. As soon as I sat down, I started crying. Saeid, too, didn't believe I would deliver that very night; after a while, he took my arms and helped me stand and walk. I was quickly getting tired and complaining to Saeid. If he had not compelled me to go to Najmiyyah Hospital, my delivery would not have been preponed so much. My walking was neither like walking nor like running. Both of them were laughing aloud and clapping for me.

After an hour, I was admitted and at 10:30 p.m., Fatemeh was born. This time we were also alone. I had told my mother that Saeid's car had broken down and we would not go to the park.

Saeid was enamored seeing Fatemeh like this! He said she was just like a snowball! He was adoring her nonstop. They brought milk for me. The date upon which I had recited the chapter Tabarak[72] was in my bag. It was said that when the syrup of this date reaches the child, she will be of a good voice. I ate the date and drank the milk. I held Fatemeh in my arms and put the *turbah*[73] on her palate. Saeid would not move his eyes off Fatemeh. "How great it would be if I were to have six daughters!" he said.

'Fatemeh' was my selection. Saeid chose 'Arifah'. He said, "You are already Zahra, and you like your daughter to be Fatemeh?" We decided that if Fatemeh had a future daughter, we would name her 'Arifah.' Fatemeh was four months old when Saeid was confined to the home. When Fatemeh used to get restless, Saeid, without saying anything, would tuck his bedding under his arms and go to the adjacent room. One of the nights when he was heading to the other room, I said, "Who was the one who wanted

---

72. Chapter Tabarak or al-Mulk is the sixty-seventh chapter of the Quran.

73. *Turbah* or Sayyid al-Shuhadah's soil or the soil of Imam al-Husayn's (a) shrine, is the soil taken from areas around the grave of Imam al-Husayn (a), the third Shiite Imam. Traditions recommend prostration on Karbala's soil or giving Karbala's soil as the first thing that a newborn consumes.

six daughters?" He said, "Please if you could handle her crying,…" and with the end of the blanket and his feet dragging on the ground, he left the room. The constant pain was visible in his eyes but never came upon his tongue. Only God knows how many times his excruciating pain was felt to the very bone, and he did not utter a single word!

Chapter 5

Sons Die and Fathers Live

It was one of the auspicious days of the month of Rajab. We had gone to the garrison. They had just distributed dinner when Muhammad Sadiq came looking for me. He did not want to attract attention. With his hands, he indicated that I should pick up Fatemeh and follow him. Saeid had a headache, one of those headaches which made him want to bite the walls! He himself sat behind the wheel in that state of pain and we returned home. We went to the doctor several times. One gave codeine and the other said it was the nerve pressure. No medicine brought about any improvement. Doctors were unable to understand what was going on in his head. My mother knew a renowned neurologist. She made an appointment for Saeid. To take Saeid, his mother and sister came to help. He did not agree to go. He was saying he couldn't stand. He was nauseated. For several days his face remained pale. We said we were going to hold him by the arms, but he did not accept. He sent them away, and they went home. Only he and I remained. I sat by him and insisted. I implored him by swearing on our children's lives. As I saw he was giving in, I called a taxi. When we arrived, the clinic was closed.

I could not manage all of his affairs by myself; if he didn't want to get up, my strength was not enough to lift him. Muhammad Sadiq also wanted to help, but his height had just reached the Saeid's waist! Only two men could rival his stubbornness: my father and his father. I called them. They came, and all three of them went to the hospital. When the doctor saw the results of his CT scan, they admitted him. They said he had to be operated on. Because I was nursing Fatemeh, they did not tell me the truth. They told me that the shell fragments in his head had gotten infected and they had to remove the infection. But Saeid had a tumor.

The doctor put him on complete bed-rest. But Saeid was his own boss. Whoever came to visit him, he would go right to the security desk to bid them farewell. He used to have arguments every night with my brother who kept him company. Every hour he would say, "Get up and go home. Now, Pari *khanum* must be speaking ill of me that I have distanced her husband from her!"

We were not able to find Saeid's medicines. I had no choice but to inform Mr. Rajabi. He didn't know that Saeid was in the hospital. He was shocked during the call. Mr. Uzamaiyan and he found Saeid's ampules. They came straight to the hospital and gave the medicines to the nurse. Majid Sayyid Hashemifar was admitted to the same hospital. He was Saeid's old friend. His symptoms from the chemical attacks had flared up. All three of them went to see him. The visitation time had ended, and I was waiting in Saeid's room. The security guard was constantly knocking on the door and notifying me that the visiting time was over. I busied myself with the nurses and patients until Saeid returned. I had promised Muhammad Sadiq that I would take permission for him from the security guard. Some hid little children under their *chadors* and would pass in front of the guard. But Muhammad Sadiq was the second man of the house; he would have been belittled under my *chador*. Since it was the last minutes of the visiting time, the guard gave permission. However, to see Fatemeh, Saeid accompanied us to the door!

For the operation, they wanted my signature and thumbprint as consent. Saeid told me on the call. I was still sitting there beside the telephone when it rang again. He had changed his mind. He said that I should send his father to give consent. He didn't want them to come to the children and me if anything happened. He explained to me in a way that would neither shock me nor make me understand the truth, by saying that after all, every operation has its risks and that life and death are in God's hands. My father-in-law went to the hospital at night and gave consent. Saeid's friends had brought a video camera and when they were shaving his head, they recorded it. My father-in-law was grieving. He was not able to bear seeing Saeid on the hospital bed. Saeid was joking with him. "Now the era is the era of the fathers; sons die and fathers live."

The operation was at 1:30 p.m. I wanted to entrust the kids to my uncle's wife at noon in order to reach the hospital before they took him to the operation room. It was not yet noon and my uncle called. The operation room had been emptied earlier and they had taken Saeid. I had not been able to meet him. I became agitated. Muhammad Sadiq was still at school and Fatemeh was in my arms. Uncle said that Saeid's mother was terribly restless. He said that I should get there as soon as possible. I froze. Definitely, something had happened, otherwise, my mother-in-law was fine up till the previous night. Everybody knew the cause of the operation except his mother and I. Before they took Saeid, the doctor had told his mother, "The risk of the operation is high. There is only a ten percent chance that we will be able to remove the tumor completely. It is possible that after the operation, he will be paralyzed or become blind." I do not remember to whom I entrusted Fatemeh. I held up my *chador* and was climbing the stairs in the hospital two steps at a time. When I arrived, they had taken him to the ICU. His friends were saying that once or twice he had opened his eyes and waved his hand at them. He had not been blinded. I found my uncle in the crowd. "Why didn't you tell me? Everybody knew but me. Am I not his wife?" Uncle's face took on a benevolent expression. "You are feeding a baby dear Zahra. We were looking after everything. And now you can see that he is doing fine."

The other side of the glass of the ICU was filled with Saeid's visitors. They were waving at him. I understood Saeid's reaction through the *salawat* and the happiness of the visitors. My turn was not going to come anytime soon! I sat on one of the free chairs in the corridor waiting. He recognized me from behind the glass. I understood that from his smile. That smile of his was the one specific for me. But very soon he made a gesture with his hands telling me to go, meaning that I should go to the kids. When the nurse understood I was his wife, they came by the window and said he was doing fine. When their hand moved towards the curtains, I asked for some more time via hand gestures. They said through gesturing, that the patients have to rest. I had a lump in my throat as I was waving goodbye to him.

I had vowed to recite the whole Quran. I took the phone and allocated a part of the Quran, to each one of the women in the family. After two or three days, he himself called home, "Hello Zahra." I descended into the chair. He had called so that I could bring his clothes for him. He didn't like the hospital clothes. I took his clothes during the visitation time.

The doctor prescribed thirty days of radiation therapy. While Saeid was wearing his formal clothes, I wore my *chador* and stopped him, imploring him to take me with him. The doctor had prohibited driving for him. But he would neither take a taxi nor take a companion with him. He would say, "Everyone has their business to attend to. Why should I trouble them?" Only a few times when there was someone to look after the kids, he allowed me to join him. On the days when he went alone, until his return, the *tasbih*[74] was in my hands! I was worried sick about him and almost died from stress. Five minutes every day, his head was under radiation. He looked fine, apparently. But his head would get heated. The hair on his head and face had become sparse. He did not have an appetite either. It seemed as if the radiation had sealed his throat. He had his special diet, but without even getting to

---

74. *Tasbih* (or *misbaha*) is a string of beads used by Muslims to enumerate their religious recitations.

the third spoon, he would leave the *sofreh*. He had turned into a bag of bones; his face was pale and his complexion forever lost its luster.

The doctor changed his medicines. The new medicines were stronger and sleep-inducing. Saeid was feeble due to the sleep-inducing pills. We couldn't go to the mosque for the Eid al-Fitr prayers. We went to my father-in-law's house. When we arrived there, they were laying out the *sofreh* for lunch. After the operation, the camera was with him everywhere. He used to gather around friends and family and quietly took pictures without revealing the real reason behind capturing them. He used to bring life, decree and fate of God as pretexts for those pictures. "If I am not around someday, let these be my memorabilia," he would say.

While his condition was not ideal, we went to the south. The guys of the EOD battalion had made a pledge, that for the day of Arafah[75] they shall all be at the garrison of

---

75. Arafah is the ninth day of Dhu l-Hijja, the last month of lunar calendar, and the day before Eid al-Adha. Special rituals have been reported for this day in hadiths, the best of which is praying and asking for

Dokouheh. We performed the *maghreb* and *isha* prayers and went to the train station. It was March, and the weather was cold. Saeid had worn the cap that he used to wear in the battle front, both as a remembrance of war and to keep the stitches warm. We were traveling with Saeid's fellow soldiers. We segregated the cabins for the men and for the women. I entrusted Muhammad Sadiq to keep me informed of his father's condition. It was the first journey for Fatemeh and she was restless. But I was only worried about Saeid. On the other hand, I was trying to lift my spirits by saying that the journey will transform his condition. I was hopeful. In Dokouheh, men and women were also separated. Men were sleeping in the administrative building and we (the women) were sleeping elsewhere. I did not go out much. In the mornings, I used to stand behind the window and wait for Saeid. I used to watch him walk. I focused on his face and searched for the pain. When his hand was playing with the cap, there was definitely something going on; it was

---

forgiveness, most of Shi'as recite the Supplication of Arafa by Imam al-Husayn (a) in the day.

either the stitches or what was underneath. When everybody left from around him, I got worried. If he were to have vertigo or nausea, someone needed to take him to a cold place. He had to lie down and take a pill. I was not by his side to give him his medicines on time. I had also entrusted his medicines to Muhammad Sadiq. The four days that we were in Dokouheh passed like four years! When we reached home, Saeid slept in those same dusty clothes. He had grown even feebler. The New Year had not yet arrived, and Imam al-Husayn (a) [76]invited him and he was granted the opportunity for pilgrimage to Iraq. I entrusted Saeid to him (a). When I was pouring water after him as a custom for bidding farewell to the traveler, I whispered, "O Sayyid al-Shuhada,[77] I seek his cure from you." I knew that Saeid himself would not ask for a cure. When they returned, it was the night before the new

---

76. Imam al-Husayn b. Ali (a), the third Shiite Imam, was the son of Imam Ali b. Abi Talib (a) and Lady Fatima al-Zahra (a). In the Shiite culture, Imam al-Husayn (a) is the symbol of martyrdom-seeking and sacrifice.

77. Sayyid al-Shuhada (literally means master of the martyrs) is one of the main titles of Imam al-Husayn (a).

year. I saw that his head and face were full of hair. My uncle said that not even once had his health deteriorated. He had recited his prayers on time and had performed all his pilgrimages. It crossed my mind that maybe he had left his pains in Karbala.

He did not have much money, yet he had brought scarves for the women and shirts for the men. He opened the suitcase of souvenirs that very night. It was his custom. Anything that he brought for us, we had to wear at that very moment. Otherwise, he would not calm down and be at rest. Out of the scarves, he separated the one whose cover was more stylish. "This is for you. It is the most expensive of them all." His perspective of colors was different from mine. He bought ten scarves, and we wanted them all. When the roll of the cloth was spread, Saeid was mesmerized by its lines and colors, as if he was behind his camera and adjusting the frame. If a color was misplaced, he would cover the lens of his camera and would not buy that cloth. When the season of caps and shawls approached, and we had wool and knitting needles in our hands, he would creatively recommend color combinations. Sometimes, he would also draw the design on paper for our knitting projects. He recognized colors accurately. He used to buy colorful stockings and ask me to wear them when he was home. He wanted our life to be colorful. But he himself always wore white, the color which had and did not have all the colors in it!

On Iranian New Year's Eve of 1381 (2002), we went to the houses of all the relatives. He was insisting on visiting all of them, distant or close, younger or elder, in the first week. I did not understand the reason behind his insisting. I was only accompanying him and looking after him.

The month of Muharram[78] was to start in the second week of the new year. Again, his mind was set on going to Dokouheh. For March 28, they booked plane tickets with some of his friends so that they could return within two to three days. They wanted to prepare Dokouheh for the speech of Ayatollah Khamenei. I explained all his medicines one by one to Mr. Rajabi. I said, "Just like your own life, take care of Saeid's

---

78. Muharram is the first month of the lunar calendar. The importance of this month is because the event of Ashura' and the martyrdom of Imam al-Husayn (a) and his companions took place in this month.

life." When they returned, I realized that he had been traveling in a warplane. Loud sounds and excessive shaking had brought back his nausea. After the holidays, we went to the doctor. My mother-in-law accompanied us. She took Fatemeh in her arms so that I could go in with Saeid. The doctor was exchanging merry courtesies with Saeid, and he was also bantering with the doctor. They were behaving as if nothing had happened. As always, he increased doses of some of the medicines, handed us the new prescription and that was all! When Saeid went out, I closed the door behind him and sat facing the doctor. I explained Saeid's condition. I said he vomits several times every day. He always feels dizzy. I said that he does not even eat as much as Muhammad Sadiq; food does not go down his throat. There is no color on his face. After taking two or three steps, he gets tired when he walks. Like this, I went on speaking. The doctor allowed me to speak about everything that I had. He was aware of my obliviousness. When I was done speaking, I tightened my *chador* below the throat and waited. The doctor leaned on the table and knitted his fingers together. He said, "Do you have the strength to hear it?" My heart sank. But I did not let the fear appear on my face. I did not want the doctor to know. I loosened the *chador* under my throat so as to swallow the lump in my throat. I nodded my head, implying that I had the strength to hear it. The doctor was speaking word by word. His words were inscribed in my mind. "Nothing more can be done," he said. "That's it? After the operation and all these medicines and treatments, that's it? Nothing more can be done?!" I said. The doctor, word by word, in the language that I could understand, explained that the tumor is malignant. They had removed the main mass which I thought to be the infection, but a malignant tumor grows back again and again. It spreads and gradually consumes the whole body, similar to an octopus surrounding its prey with its arms. "Pray for him and seek his cure from God. Only a miracle can restore him," the doctor said.

When I stood up from the chair, I felt lethargic. My whole body felt very heavy upon my legs. I threw my hand on the doorknob but it did not open. Through my wet eyes, I saw two door knobs! I closed my eyes. Behind the door were my mother-in-law and Fatemeh. There was Saeid, and it was uncertain until when he would be among us. I didn't want his mother to know.

I took a deep breath and gulped down the lump in my throat. I rolled my index finger into my *chador* and dried my eyes. I turned the knob and went out of the room. My mother-in-law had a concerned look in her eyes. I dodged my eyes from hers and turned to Saeid. "The doctor said that you should not have gone to the South. You should not have been in an airplane, let alone a warplane. Hadn't he prohibited it?! "Till when will you listen only to yourself?" I had cooked lunch the night before. I entrusted Fatemeh to my mother so that I could heat up the food. My throat was hurting because of the choking feeling I had developed since receiving the news. Mother left after lunch. Pretending to want to put Fatemeh to sleep, I went into the room and closed the door. I put a pillow on my legs and rocked and rocked Fatemeh. Father and daughter went to sleep quickly. I just wanted to scream and cry out. The situation, however, was beyond crying and wailing. The telephone rang. As soon as I heard the voice of Mr. Uzamaiyan, I burst into tears. The poor guy did not know how to calm me down! I told him, "Let's take him abroad for treatment." He said that they had tried everything. He had done a lot of research. It was not about the expertise and the equipment. Saeid's illness had progressed so much that nobody could have done anything. "Entrust him to God. Whatever God wills shall happen," he said. When I hung up the phone, Saeid had already woken up. "It was one of my friends," I said. He would get displeased if I had cried in front of a *non-mahram*.

We had brought a bed. One of those hospital beds which move up and down with the touch of a button. Now he was just sleeping in bed. The bed had become a toy for the kids. Either they made the bed a house and went under it or they chased each other around it. In the beginning, I did not get in their way. They were entertained by it, as was Saeid. I had not told him that I was aware of his illness. I drove away negative thoughts from my mind. I wanted to take a picture of each of his days, but he would come to know that something was up. I wanted to look at him more and talk to him more. I used to sit on the edge of the bed and caress his head. I had memorized the supplication of curing the sick from *Mafatih*.[79] I used to recite it seven times and

---

79. *Mafatih al-Jinan* is a book containing supplications, major Shiite worships, and *ziyara* (pilgrimage

blow on him. Chemotherapy drugs made his facial hair fall out. I was not letting him know and tidying up his beard. I kissed his sunken cheeks and adored him.

When my parents came to visit, he would tell them that he had been stuck in the house and all the trouble had fallen upon my shoulders. He would kiss my hands and face and show gratitude. I used to say, "This is my duty, you pray. Eventually, it is you who should seek to be cured." If anyone saw in a dream that he was cured, they would call to tell me. I could not think of him not being there, even for a moment. All my thoughts and feelings were focused on him staying alive. I flew to the future, ours and our children's future. I pledged a vow and recited the Quran. Every time he got up from the bed and went from one room to the other, I thanked Allah that he was still up and moving. When he used to get bored, he would take the album in his hands. He used to arrange his photos and would write

---

supplications) of the Prophet's Household (a), which Shaykh Abbas Qummi collected about one hundred years ago. Today, Mafatih is the best-known book of supplications among Shias and can be found in most homes.

dates on them. But when he used to pick up a book, my heart would tremble. His eyesight was not as strong as before. He followed the small words of the book and got nauseated. After a few times, he learned what to do. He read one or two pages and put it down. In the end, those very eyes caused him trouble. The doctor said that if he was not operated on again, he would lose his eyesight. He was hospitalized again.

They wanted to anesthetize him, and the doctor said he might not regain consciousness after the operation. When his father heard this, he took back his consent. He had become restless. His face turned pale, and his temperature decreased. Saeid came back out wearing the clothes of the operation room. He took his father's hands and looked right into his eyes. "Why did you not let them operate on me, Dad? If it's my time to die, then let me die and mourn over me once, rather than mourning over me every day. Why did you make me return to this place again?" The operation was postponed. The hospital was quite boring for him. He would get up and visit other patients. He gave them water, changed television channels for them, and became a conversation mate for them. He lifted the spirits of everybody around him. Even my spirits too. "What are you worried about?" he asked. I was worried about him. He had to get better to make Muhammad Sadiq a groom. Fatemeh's daughter must listen to the story of her name from her grandfather. We hadn't been to many places yet. What will happen to *hajj*? He had promised that we were to go together once for *hajj*. The ten years of our married life had not yet been filled. It was too early for him to leave.

I had asked the doctor about his diet; I used to cook and take the food to the hospital. I used to cook chicken, quail and partridge; he would eat its cuttings. The academic year was coming to its end and I had to take care of Muhammad Sadiq's lessons. Fatemeh, too, had grown and wanted a companion to play with. She tore apart Muhammad Sadiq's book and notebook if I was not watching after her. On the days I knew I would not be able to go during visiting hours, I passed gave Saeid's food to his friends to take to him.

Eventually, we took the consent of Saeid's father. When they were taking him from the operating room to the ICU, it was not like the previous time. He neither opened his eyes nor waved his hand at anyone. I felt like I had lost all support. I took Fatemeh from my mother and held her to my chest. Fatemeh was able to comfort me. The next day when he called home, I was stuttering on the phone! He said that he had been transferred from the ICU to the ward. He again wanted his own clothes. He remained in the ward one to two days and due to his insistence, he was discharged. My uncle came after me. I put his clothes in a sack, and we started heading toward the hospital. On our way to the hospital, I realized I had not packed his trousers. Uncle stopped the car at an *Etka* store and went to buy a pair. He bought very loose pants because he did not know Saeid's size. When handing over Saeid's clothes, I kept the pants for last. When the folds of the pants opened and the pleats of the pants became visible, he started laughing aloud. I said, "Well, you have no idea what condition I was in." We laughed a lot until we reached the car. We had all forgotten as to where we were and for what we had come!

Saeid's parents stayed with us for a few nights. At dawn, when I wanted to wake them up for the prayers, I saw that the lights in their room were on. I opened the door a bit. His father was on the prayer mat. From the movements of his shoulders, I understood that he was crying. He was sitting with his legs folded, and his arms were raised towards the heavens. "O Allah, reduce my age and increase the lifespan of my son. I am entrusting my Saeid to You," he said, sobbingly. It was what he did every day. When he bent down to open the prayer mat, his tears would fall on the carpet. He used to sob and speak to Allah. He had become thin out of worrying for Saeid.

I used to quickly finish the chores of the house, so that I could spend more time with Saeid. Several times a day, I used to place a chair beside his bed and would look at him. If he was sleeping, I opened *Mafatih* and recited some prayers. I would follow the curve of his eyebrows from the middle of the forehead until close to the temples. The capillary vessels which were apparent below his eyelids. His lips which had cracked due to dryness. Sometimes I saw that he had opened his eyes and was watching me in silence. I tried to act normally. "Did you sleep well?" I asked him. One night he brought up the issue of the children. "Take care of the kids. Do not let them fall behind in their studies and homework. Do not let them catch a cold in winter and have heat stroke in the summer. Take care of yourself too. You are the decision-maker of the family. Make whatever decision you think is suitable for your life. Forgive my shortcomings." My face became full of tears. He wiped my tears with his thin, long fingers and kissed my forehead. He used to kiss my and the children's faces every opportunity he got. Anybody who saw him would not have believed that this was the same shy Saeid from the beginning of our married life. Day and night he was in the house, and every moment I missed him.

It was the peak of broad beans season. I had purchased ten kilos of broad beans and was busy cleaning them. Saeid developed a desire for cooked broad beans. I separated the tiny beans which cooked faster and poured them into a pot. When he woke up from his afternoon nap, I put oregano and vinegar in it and took it for him. He was eating, and instead of saying 'wow' and 'great,' he was complaining, "These are so tiny." I told him, "The big ones take time to cook. I will cook the bigger ones for the next batch." Suddenly, the doorbell rang. It was my uncle. "Saeid's father passed away," he said. I froze up. He had died out of anguish for his son. A cold sweat settled on my back. Saeid had finished the broad beans and had lied down on the bed. He was not attentive to me. I opened the door for my uncle, but the receiver of the intercom was still held against my ear. My heart was beating fast. My mind had jammed. My hands and feet too. Only Saeid's words were repeating in my head: "Now the era is the era of fathers. Sons die, and fathers live."

I opened the apartment door and ran towards the bathroom. I was crying and washing my face. However, the more water I was throwing at my face, the redness of my eyes increased. When I stepped out of the bathroom, my uncle was sitting beside Saeid's bed. Saeid had again gone to sleep. We went into the room so that nobody heard our voices. The next day was the funeral procession of my father-in-law. The doctor had not allowed us to tell Saeid. So, I stayed home as if not even a leaf had fallen off a tree![80] As if it was a day like any other day of God! The only thing we did was that when my uncle was leaving, he severed the telephone cable from downstairs. Our pretext was, for instance, that they

---

80. As if not even a leaf had fallen off a tree is a Persian allegory meaning that nothing has happened.

were changing the cables and everyone's telephones were disconnected!

The day after the burial, my mother-in-law came. She had worn navy blue. When she was exchanging pleasantries with Saeid, her voice was gruff. She said she had caught a cold. She had caught a cold due to the heat of the end of spring! We went to the kitchen, and we both burst into tears. We embraced each other and our eyes rained down like spring clouds. She was not calming down. I had lost the words. What should I have said to someone whose husband had recently been buried and her son was dying before her eyes?! Someone should have thought of a solution for my own problem first! Our Saeid was bedridden and nothing could have been done by anyone.

Saeid insisted that his mother should stay with us for lunch. His mother was the host for the mourners. Flocks of people were coming to their house to offer their condolences. She had to go. She said, "Haj Agha (your father) is alone. I have to go and give him lunch." For the mourning program of the third day, after the demise of my father-in-law, we devised a plan with my uncle. I said to Saeid that they had taken my grandfather to the hospital, and I asked his permission to go and visit him. "Allah had returned your grandfather from the brink of death a few times before." Saeid said, "This time also his God is great. God willing, he will get well." He asked me to stay. He needed me.

Saeid's friends were coming from his father's funeral to meet him. I was standing at the door and to each one of them, I explained that Saeid was still unaware of his father's death. Until the time the last one of them left, my heart skipped a beat a thousand times. I feared that a word might slip their tongues, and they would offer condolences! When Mr. Uzamaiyan came, I entrusted Saeid to him. I found a cozy corner and cried to my fill, far from the eyes of Saeid and the children.

We told him after two weeks. It was Friday. Mr. Rajabi and Mr. Uzamaiyan came and took Saeid to the *imamzadeh*.[81] My heart was not at rest. What if he had to be taken to the hospital? What if he suffered a

---

81. *Imamzadeh* is the descendant of an infallible Imam who is often particularly respected by Shias, because of their lineage to the Imam, and domes and shrines are built on their tombs.

convulsion? The phone rang. It was Saeid. Teardrops gathered under my chin and rolled down upon my skirt. "Condolences to you, *agha* Saeid. May Allah bestow forgiveness upon Haj Agha," I said. "I owe you... I will come home and settle my account with you too." He was not furious. He was calm. I could see his smile on the other side of the phone. He stayed the night at his mother's. After that, whenever his mother came, he used to hide her shoes. "Haj Agha is not here anymore. Who will you bring as an excuse for not staying?" Her excuse was Saeid. His mother didn't have the strength to sit and watch her son's pain. A bereaved mother is much worse. Until the fortieth day of the demise, she used to come and visit us, but would not stay long. Saeid's condition was getting worse and worse.

It was June. The schools were closed, and Muhammad Sadiq was home. However much he wanted to be considerate, he was a boy, and was quite naughty after all. I sent Saeid to his mother's house. I thought that his mother would not be lonely and Saeid, too, would be able to rest in silence. I also took the kids to the yard and playpark of our residential complex for them to play. He called the next day. "Come. Let us go to Haj Agha's grave." It was my first time visiting it. A few meters away, there was a memorial. They were reciting *rozeh*.[82] What a *rozeh* it was! I burst into tears. I was crying for Haj Agha, and I was crying for myself. My pain had piled up layers upon layers. Saeid's pain was the heaviest. Saeid had picked up a pebble, knocking it upon the grave like a sparrow picking the grains. He was not weeping. He had asked us that we should not weep for him either. He was ready to die. Sometimes, when he would sleep on the floor, I brought him a pillow and blanket and woke him up. He used to say, "Here, you take care of me and place a pillow under my head; tomorrow, when they put my head upon the cold earth, where would the pillow be? In these two days of this world also, let me put my head upon the earth so that maybe my head will get used to the hardness."

He was missing the kids. It was barely two days, and he called, so we went and brought him back.

---

82. *Rozeh* is a mourning practice in which the tragedy of Imam al-Husayn (a) and other Infallibles (a) are recited.

We could not attend the chehellom[83] of his father. He did not have the strength to stand. His heart wanted to go but he could not move his feet off the ground. When the fortieth passed, he became bedridden and never got up again. I begged the doctor to admit him, but Saeid was not allowing it. He used to say that the hospital and home are the same for him. Most of the time he was asleep. One night we all gathered with friends and relatives and recited Ziyara Ashura next to him. He was watching the people but did not show any reaction. One of his friends had booked tickets to Mashhad for us. We gave back the tickets as Saeid was not feeling well anymore; he could not recall people and memories. The summer arrived, along with big and bloody blisters. When I used to put his shirt on, the blisters would burst, and tears would flow from the corners of his eyes. Over and under him, I had put white bed sheets. When I took Fatemeh to him, she would extend her hands toward the blisters. When once or twice I pulled her hands back, Saeid objected. "Let her touch, maybe my pain will decrease."

---

83. Fortieth or chehellom is a ceremony held on the fortieth day after a person's death.

Chapter 6

Patience, Lady Zaynab's(a) Gift

Saeid's sister Zahra had come to visit him. We had laid out the *sofreh* on the ground beside the bed. His sister was making very small morsels and putting them in his mouth. A morsel got caught in his throat. He started coughing. The coughing increased his pain. His face had turned black and blue. He was choking. His sister ran into the yard and sought help. The emergency ambulance came fast. His lungs had an infection. The EMT with the ambulance said that he should be admitted. "Well, take him to the hospital with this very ambulance," I said. However, they did not take him. They said that their duty was only to perform the check-up. We called the

IRGC's hospital. "We do not have any empty beds," they said. I begged. I cried. They said, "It is not possible." Muhammad Sadiq was in the yard. When he came up, Saeid's throat was still growling. Muhammad Sadiq started crying. He was crying and hitting his feet on the ground. Zahra, Saeid's sister said, "I have no more strength to lose this one!" Her husband had been martyred, she had lost her father a few days ago, and now it was Saeid. She said we should take him to Mustafa Khomeini hospital. It was the hospital of Bonyad-e Shahid.[84] We called; they sent an ambulance. Saeid was taken. All were gone. The kids and I remained with an empty bed!

At night, Saeid called. He had asked them to dial the home number and to give the phone to him. He asked about the kids and me and how we were doing. He was well, as if a miracle had happened. The fact that he was aware of us and had

---

84. Bonyad-e Shahid or Foundation of Martyrs and Veterans Affairs is a governmental institution that was established after the victory of the Islamic Revolution in Iran at the command of Imam Khomeini to support veterans, those injured in the war, and families of martyrs in Iran.

called to stop us from worrying meant that a miracle had happened. The next day again, we recited Ziyara Ashura. The men were around the empty bed, and the women were in the room. I could not reach the hospital during visiting hours.

On Wednesday, I entrusted the kids to my mother and visited him. "How are you, dear Saeid?" I asked. "*Alhamdulillah*,"[85] he said. Then he started reciting the chapter of al-Fateha.[86] I was reminded of his last prayers. I used to take water by his bed. He had forgotten how to perform ablution (*wudhu*). I used to help him perform ablution. The blisters would pass one by one under my fingers. If any of them would burst, I used to clean its bloody liquid and would give him *wudhu* again from the start. He would give up reciting al-Fateha and another chapter in the middle and go into prostration. I asked about the validity of his prayer and was told there was no problem.

---

85. Alhamdulillah is an Arabic phrase meaning "praise be to God," sometimes translated as "thank God."
86. Chapter al-Fateha or al-Hamd is the first chapter of the Quran. It is recommended to recite it when visiting a sick person.

His prayer was accepted in whatever way he performed it. "*Ihdina al-sirat al-mustaqim...*,"[87] He started breathing fast. He was opening and closing his mouth like a fish in a pitcher. The air was not reaching him. The nurses came, and we went out. They put the oxygen mask on him. When his condition became stable, they again took him to the ICU. My mother called. Fatemeh continuously badgered her to see me. But I could not detach my heart from there. They called again, and I returned home. Saeid regained consciousness that night. They said he called upon Hazrat Abu al-fadhl (a)[88] three times and went into a coma. Four days later, it was Fatemeh's first birthday. She did not understand these things at that point. She did not yet have a picture of Saeid in her mind. But I took Muhammad Sadiq to visit. He was scared of the wires and pipes that were attached to his father. He walked

---

87. "*Ihdina al-sirat al-mustaqim*" is the transliteration of one of the verses of Chapter al-Fateha, which means 'Guide us to the right path'.

88. Hazrat Abu al-fadhl (a) or al-Abbas (a), was the son of Imam Ali (a) and Umm al-Baneen. He was the commander and flagbearer of Imam al-Husayn's army in the Event of Karbala.

towards his father, kissed him, and quickly ran out. I recited the Quran by his side. I used to recite the supplication of Mi'raj. I used to recite chapter al-Tawhid seven times and blow. I had heard that this particular chapter brings about miracles. I would recite whatever I knew. There was nothing I could do. I only knew these things. When a visitor came by, I would wipe my face and go out. The doctors said that he was brain dead. He was showing no reactions. It was the night of July 11. The phone rang. A person had seen a dream whereby a man in white clothes had come to Saeid's bedside and kissed his forehead. We became certain that Saeid would not return.

When the sound of "*Allahu akbar*" rose from the mosque, I performed *wudhu*. "*Hayya alas-salaah ...*," I set out the prayer mat. I wanted to go and visit Saeid after the prayers. The phone rang. "*Hayya ala l-falaah ...*," my sister picked up the call. "*Hayya ala khayri l-amal*[89]," she started crying. My Saeid had been martyred. "*Allahu akbar ... Allahu akbar*," I stood up and burst into tears.

When we were living in the Tolid Daroo neighborhood, one of my friends

---

89. These are the *adhan's* phrases.

had a daughter named Zahra. She was a playmate of Muhammad Sadiq. She was seven or eight months younger than Muhammad Sadiq, but in the mosque, she used to point out the Quranic mistakes of the women. After the martyrdom of Saeid, Zahra saw a dream of Karbala. She had told her mother, "They were taking the captives. Muhammad Sadiq's mother was also there. Lady Zaynab (a)[90] came and gave something to Muhammad Sadiq's mother." It was PATIENCE. When the news of his martyrdom reached me, right there, in my prayers, I had asked for patience.

At night we went to Mi'raj-e Shuhada.[91] They had arranged a program for Saeid and three unidentified martyrs. Saeid's face was visible. They had placed a cloth under his head, and it had been elevated. I didn't take my eyes off him. All around the coffins, they

---

90. Lady Zaynab (626-682) was the daughter of Imam Ali (a) and Lady Fatimah (a). She accompanied her brother Imam al-Husayn (a) in the Event of Karbala, and after the martyrdom of the Imam and his companions, she and the other women and children were captured by the Umayyad army.

91. Mi'raj-e Shuhada is the place where the corpses of martyrs are kept before they are buried.

had arranged geranium flower pots. Besides the flowerpots, white candles were also lit up. In the end, I was also unable to watch him to my fill. They showed his face for a few moments, and that was it. For his funeral procession, the crowd was so big that I didn't even understand when they recited *talqin*[92] over him and when they put the stone to close the grave. However, Muhammad Sadiq saw everything. He didn't yet know that his father had been martyred. I had entrusted others to keep him busy outside Mi'raj-e Shuhada. I don't know how he escaped from their hands and came in. He had seen Saeid and was crying out, "This is my father... my father." He had gotten frightened from seeing the coffins. He was not calming down in anyone's embrace. That very night he had a seizure.

When Saeid left, Fatemeh turned two years old. After four months, when we had gone to Mecca with my mother-in-law and the kids, one of the caravan's women, with

---

92. *Talqin* consists of *dhikrs* or reminders about Islamic beliefs (monotheism, prophethood, resurrection, imamate, etc.), which is recited over a dead body before its burial in a particular manner. It is recommended to recite *talqin* for the dead.

whom I had recently become friends, saw a dream that Saeid was sitting right there beside me and had taken Fatemeh into his embrace. He craved to see her walk so much. Now when Fatemeh sees anybody in the street with an IRGC uniform, she runs, saying, "Dad, Dad." I have recently taught her that she should call them uncle. Now she also addresses Saeid's picture as uncle!

I see him a lot in my dreams. One night, when I was very restless, I saw him in a dream. He said, "Don't worry, dear Zahra. I am always by your side."

When we go with the kids to his grave, Muhammad Sadiq first washes the stone with rosewater. Then, he arranges the flowers on the stone one by one. He does not remove the petals of the flowers. In the beginning, when the grave was yet to have a stone, and we poured water on the soil, he used to shout, "Don't pour water. Don't pour water." We thought that he feared Saeid getting wet. But Muhammad Sadiq was concerned about the ants. He said, "The ants will get wet." Muhammad Sadiq was concerned about ants, and I was worried about his and Fatimah's future. Every time I wipe the frame of Saeid's photo, I ask him for help for the sake of the kids.

"Muhammad Sadiq's exams have begun. Tomorrow, he has spelling. I have promised him that if he gets full marks, I will buy him Gorji zoo biscuits. I will say that they are from you. Forgive me."

I open the door of his cupboard to organize it. Then I say, what if he comes back suddenly and complains? Let me close it. If he returns and says, "Again, you have misplaced my albums?" What answer will I give him? I will let him come and organize his room himself.

www.ingramcontent.com/pod-product-compliance
Lightning Source LLC
Chambersburg PA
CBHW030042100526
44590CB00011B/297